Python Programming For All

An Easy and Comprehensive Guide To Learn Python Programming Language

© Written By John P Newton

like anything else in life, there are no guarantees of results. Readers are cautioned to rely on their own judgment about their individual circumstances and act accordingly.

This book is not intended for use as a source of legal, medical, business, accounting or financial advice. All readers are advised to seek services of competent professionals in the legal, medical, business, accounting, and finance fields.

Table of Contents

Introduction

Python is a computer programming language that lets you work more quickly than can pick up Python very quickly, and beginners find the clean syntax and indentation structure easy to learn. This tutorial will help you to become a python developer.

The Evolution of Python Language Over the Years

According to several websites, Python is one of the most popular coding languages of 2017. Along with being a high-level and general-purpose programming language, Python is also object-oriented and open source. At the same time, a good number of developers across the world have been making use of Python to create GUI applications, websites and mobile apps. The differentiating factor that Python brings to the table is that it enables programmers to flesh out concepts by writing less and readable code. The developers can further take advantage of several Python frameworks to mitigate the time and effort required for building large and complex software applications.

The programming language is currently being used by a number of high-traffic websites including Google, Yahoo Groups, Yahoo Maps, Linux Weekly News, Shopzilla and Web Therapy. Likewise, Python also finds great use for creating gaming, financial, scientific and educational applications. However, developers still use different versions of the programming language. According to the usage statistics and market share data of Python posted on W3techs, currently Python 2 is being used by 99.4% of websites, whereas Python 3 is being used only by 0.6% of websites. That is why, it becomes essential for each programmer to understand different versions of Python, and its evolution over many years.

How Python Has Been Evolving over the Years?

Conceived as a Hobby Programming Project

Despite being one of the most popular coding languages of 2015, Python was originally conceived by Guido van Rossum as a hobby project in December 1989. As Van Rossum's office remained closed during Christmas, he was looking for a hobby project that will keep him occupied during the holidays. He planned to create an interpreter for a new scripting language, and named the project as Python. Thus, Python was originally designed as a successor to ABC programming language. After writing the interpreter, Van Rossum made the code public in February 1991. However, at present the open source programming language is being managed by the Python Software Foundation.

Version 1 of Python

Python 1.0 was released in January 1994. The major release included a number of new features and functional programming tools including lambda, filter, map and reduce. The version 1.4 was released with several new features like keyword arguments, built-in support for complex numbers, and a basic form of data hiding. The major release was followed by two minor releases, version 1.5 in December 1997 and version 1.6 in September 2000. The version 1 of Python lacked the features offered by popular programming languages of the time. But the initial versions created a solid foundation for development of a powerful and futuristic programming language.

Version 2 of Python

In October 2000, Python 2.0 was released with the new list comprehension feature and a garbage collection system. The syntax for the list comprehension feature was inspired by other functional programming languages like Haskell. But Python 2.0, unlike Haskell, gave preference to alphabetic keywords over punctuation characters. Also, the garbage collection system effectuated collection of reference cycles. The major release was followed by several minor releases. These releases added a number of functionality to the programming language like support for nested scopes, and unification of Python's classes and types into a single hierarchy. The Python Software Foundation has already announced that there would be no Python 2.8. However, the Foundation will provide support to version 2.7 of thc programming language till 2020.

Version 3 of Python

Python 3.0 was released in December 2008. It came with a several new features and enhancements, along with a number of deprecated features. The deprecated features and backward incompatibility make version 3 of Python completely different from earlier versions. So many developers still use Python 2.6 or 2.7 to avail the features deprecated from last major release. However, the new features of Python 3 made it more modern and popular. Many developers even switched to version 3.0 of the programming language to avail these awesome features.

Python 3.0 replaced print statement with the built-in print() function, while allowing programmers to use custom separator between lines. Likewise, it simplified the rules of ordering comparison. If the operands are not organized in a natural and meaningful order, the ordering comparison operators can now raise a TypeError exception. The version 3 of the programming language further uses text and data instead of Unicode and 8-bit strings. While treating all code as Unicode by default it represents binary data as encoded Unicode.

As Python 3 is backward incompatible, the programmers cannot access features like string exceptions, old-style classes, and implicit relative imports. Also, the developers must be familiar with changes made to syntax and APIs. They can use a tool called "2to3" to migrate their application from Python 2 to 3 smoothly. The tool highlights incompatibility and areas of concern through comments and warnings. The comments help programmers to make changes to the code, and upgrade their existing applications to the latest version of programming language.

Latest Versions of Python

At present, programmers can choose either version 3.4.3 or 2.7.10 of Python. Python 2.7 enables developers to avail improved numeric handling and enhancements for standard library. The version further makes it easier for developers to migrate to Python 3. On the other hand, Python 3.4 comes with several new features and library modules, security improvements and CPython implementation improvements. However, a number of features are deprecated in both Python API and programming language. The developers can still use Python 3.4 to avail support in the longer run.

Version 4 of Python

Python 4.0 is expected to be available in 2023 after the release of Python 3.9. It will come with features that will help programmers to switch from version 3 to 4 seamlessly. Also, as they gain experience, the expert Python developers can take advantage of a number of backward compatible features to modernize their existing applications without putting any extra time and effort. However, the developers still have to wait many years to get a clear picture of Python 4.0. However, they must monitor the latest releases to easily migrate to the version 4.0 of the popular coding language.

The version 2 and version 3 of Python are completely different from each other. So each programmer must understand the features of these distinct versions, and compare their functionality based on specific needs of the project. Also, he needs to check the version of Python that each framework supports. However, each developer must take advantage of the latest version of Python to avail new features and long-term support.

Python Development and Its Distinguishing Features

Who Can Make Use of the Program?

Different people with a wide range of backgrounds, ages and educational levels are involved in Python development today. You can become one of them, no matter whether you are a student, a computer designer, a housewife, or a retiree. There is always a number of thorough instructions to make your introduction into the matter easier, and your success more sustainable. You can find a lot of them in the Internet. Here, you may just get acquainted with some starting points and stepping stones of the process.

The First Steps

To begin with, you will need to download the Python source and its code. For better source control, the development team applies the Subversion of the most updated modification of every file in the project. The free online book entitled "Version Control with Subversion" will help you to get more detailed information on the Subversion.

If you want to start Python development on Windows, download also Microsoft Studio 2008, or just its free version called Express. If you use UNIX-like systems (Mac, Linux or others), you will have to install some special tools through your package manager. To start running Python, you will need to identify the type of the platform to be able to invoke the interpreter in different manners. After the process of complete installation is finished, you may start working.

What Do You Need to Know?

Use PEP-7 and PEP-8 tools as useful guides for the Python codebase to ensure you are on the same page with anybody else. Always test your work when you change the code. You may find appropriate tests for each module in the test directory. As many people are working together with you simultaneously, they can see your stages of development. So, consider code reviews and comments a helpful means for writing a better code. This will also help you to stay away from bugs.

The most interesting thing in the whole process of Python development is its new features. They should be available with the corresponding documentation and code explanations. Try to write as much useful information as it is possible. Even if you don't feel comfortable with the Python documentation, there is always a person who will be able to help you with the format. Always test new features before you get your work accepted. Creating a patch is the next step to make your feature available for the core development team. You may use the "diff" command in your Subversion to generate this patch.

How to Promote Your Achievements?

If you want everybody to know what you have done, write a good comment for an issue, or upload the patch. There are different fields within which you may classify your patches to attract different groups of people. Sometimes, it takes from weeks to months for the issue to be understood by core developers. Just one person needs to review the codes of the patches to make sure of the codebase quality. Try to be available for comments or even for some criticism about your work. It is likely to be accepted quicker if you are able to react fast and openly to possible suggestions.

In fact, Python development is a sort of education and rewarding experience as well as the way to expand some knowledge while providing the community with service. We hope that this short piece of advice will help you to make as much contribution to your social environment as possible.

Python is available on a wide variety of platforms including Linux and Mac OS X. Let's understand how to set up our Python environment.

Local Environment Setup

Open a terminal window and type "python" to find out if it is already installed and which version is installed.

Unix (Solaris, Linux, FreeBSD, AIX, HP/UX, SunOS, IRIX, etc.)
Win 9x/NT/2000
Macintosh (Intel, PPC, 68K)
OS/2
DOS (multiple versions)
PalmOS
Nokia mobile phones
Windows CE
Acorn/RISC OS
BeOS
Amiga
VMS/OpenVMS
QNX
VxWorks
Psion

Python has also been ported to the Java and .NET virtual machines

Getting Python

The most up-to-date and current source code, binaries, documentation, news, etc., is available on the official website of Python https://www.python.org/

You can download Python documentation from https://www.python.org/doc/. The documentation is available in HTML, PDF, and PostScript formats.

Installing Python

Python distribution is available for a wide variety of platforms. You need to download only the binary code applicable for your platform and install Python.

If the binary code for your platform is not available, you need a C compiler to compile the source code manually. Compiling the source code offers more flexibility in terms of choice of features that you require in your installation.

Here is a quick overview of installing Python on various platforms -

Unix and Linux Installation

Here are the simple steps to install Python on Unix/Linux machine.

Open a Web browser and go to https://www.python.org/downloads.

Follow the link to download zipped source code available for Unix/Linux.

Download and extract files.

Editing the Modules/Setup file if you want to customize some options.

run ./configure script

make

make install

This installs Python at standard location /usr/local/bin and its libraries at /usr/local/lib/pythonXX where XX is the version of Python.

Windows Installation

Here are the steps to install Python on Windows machine.

Open a Web browser and go to www.python.org/downloads

Follow the link for the Windows installer python-XYZ.msi file where XYZ is the version you need to install.

To use this installer python-XYZ.msi, the Windows system must support Microsoft Installer 2.0. Save the installer file to your local machine and then run it to find out if your machine supports MSI.

Run the downloaded file. This brings up the Python install wizard, which is really easy to use. Just accept the default settings, wait until the install is finished, and you are done.

Macintosh Installation

Recent Macs come with Python installed, but it may be several years out of date. See http://www.python.org/download/mac/ for instructions on getting the current version along with extra tools to support development on the Mac. For older Mac OS's before Mac OS X 10.3 (released in 2003), MacPython is available.

Jack Jansen maintains it and you can have full access to the entire documentation at his website - http://www.cwi.nl/~jack /macpython.html. You can find complete installation details for Mac OS installation.

Setting up PATH

Programs and other executable files can be in many directories, so operating systems provide a search path that lists the directories that the OS searches for executables.

The path is stored in an environment variable, which is a named string maintained by the operating system. This variable contains information available to the command shell and other programs.

The path variable is named as PATH in Unix or Path in Windows (Unix is casesensitive; Windows is not).

In Mac OS, the installer handles the path details. To invoke the Python interpreter from any particular directory, you must add the Python directory to your path.

Setting path at Unix/Linux

To add the Python directory to the path for a particular session in Unix -

In the csh shell - type setenv PATH "$PATH:/usr/local/bin/python" and press Enter.

In the bash shell (Linux) - type export ATH="$PATH:/usr/local/bin/python" and press Enter.

In the sh or ksh shell - type PATH="$PATH:/usr/local/bin/python" and press Enter.

Note - /usr/local/bin/python is the path of the Python directory

Setting path at Windows

To add the Python directory to the path for a particular session in Windows -

At the command prompt - type path %path%;C:\Python and press Enter.

Note - C:\Python is the path of the Python directory

Python Environment Variables

Here are important environment variables, which can be recognized by Python -

S.No. Variable & Description

1

PYTHONPATH

It has a role similar to PATH. This variable tells the Python interpreter where to locate the module files imported into a program. It should include the Python source library directory and the directories containing Python source code. PYTHONPATH is sometimes preset by the Python installer.

2

PYTHONSTARTUP

It contains the path of an initialization file containing Python source code. It is executed every time you start the interpreter. It is named as .pythonrc.py in Unix and it contains commands that load utilities or modify PYTHONPATH.

3
PYTHONCASEOK

It is used in Windows to instruct Python to find the first case-insensitive match in an import statement. Set this variable to any value to activate it.

4
PYTHONHOME

It is an alternative module search path. It is usually embedded in the PYTHONSTARTUP or PYTHONPATH directories to make switching module libraries easy.

Running Python

There are three different ways to start Python -

Interactive Interpreter

You can start Python from Unix, DOS, or any other system that provides you a command-line interpreter or shell window.

Enter python the command line.

Start coding right away in the interactive interpreter.

$python # Unix/Linux
or
python% # Unix/Linux
or
C:> python # Windows/DOS

Python Basic Operators

Operators are the constructs which can manipulate the value of operands.

Consider the expression 4 + 5 = 9. Here, 4 and 5 are called operands and + is called operator.

Types of Operator

Python language supports the following types of operators.

Arithmetic Operators

Comparison (Relational) Operators

Assignment Operators

Logical Operators

Bitwise Operators

Membership Operators

Identity Operators

Let us have a look on all operators one by one.

Python Operators Precedence

The following table lists all operators from highest precedence to lowest.

Operator	Description
**	Exponentiation (raise to the power)
~ + -	Complement, unary plus and minus (method names for the last two are +@ and -@)
* / % //	Multiply, divide, modulo and floor division
+ -	Addition and subtraction
>> <<	Right and left bitwise shift
&	Bitwise 'AND'
^ |	Bitwise exclusive `OR' and regular `OR'
<= < > >=	Comparison operators
<> == !=	Equality operators
= %= /= //= -= += *= **=	Assignment operators is is not
	Identity operators in not in
	Membership operators not or and
	Logical operators

Python Decision Making

Decision making is anticipation of conditions occurring while execution of the program and specifying actions taken according to the conditions.

Decision structures evaluate multiple expressions which produce TRUE or FALSE as outcome. You need to determine which action to take and which statements to execute if outcome is TRUE or FALSE otherwise.

Following is the general form of a typical decision making structure found in most of the programming languages -

Python programming language assumes any non-zero and non-null values as TRUE, and if it is either zero or null, then it is assumed as FALSE value.

Python programming language provides following types of decision making statements.

Single Statement Suites

If the suite of an if clause consists only of a single line, it may go on the same line as the header statement.

Here is an example of a one-line if clause -

```
#!/usr/bin/python

var = 100

if ( var  == 100 ) : print "Value of expression is 100"
```

Python Loops

In general, statements are executed sequentially: The first statement in a function is executed first, followed by the second, and so on. There may be a situation when you need to execute a block of code several number of times.

Programming languages provide various control structures that allow for more complicated execution paths.

A loop statement allows us to execute a statement or group of statements multiple times.

Python programming language provides following types of loops to handle looping requirements.

Loop Type Description
while loop

Repeats a statement or group of statements while a given condition is TRUE. It tests the condition before executing the loop body.
for loop

Executes a sequence of statements multiple times and abbreviates the code that manages the loop variable.
nested loops

You can use one or more loop inside any another while, for or do.. while loop.

Loop Control Statements

Loop control statements change execution from its normal sequence. When execution leaves a scope, all automatic objects that were created in that scope are destroyed.

Python Numbers

Number data types store numeric values. They are immutable data types, means that changing the value of a number data type results in a newly allocated object.

Number objects are created when you assign a value to them. For example -

```
var1 = 1
var2 = 10
```

You can also delete the reference to a number object by using the del statement. The syntax of the del statement is -

```
del var1[,var2[,var3[....,varN]]]]
```

You can delete a single object or multiple objects by using the del statement. For example:

```
del var
del var_a, var_b
```

Python supports four different numerical types -

int (signed integers): They are often called just integers or ints, are positive or negative whole numbers with no decimal point.

long (long integers): Also called longs, they are integers of unlimited size, written like integers and followed by an uppercase or lowercase L.

float (floating point real values) : Also called floats, they represent real numbers and are written with a decimal point dividing the integer and fractional parts. Floats may also be in scientific notation, with E or e indicating the power of 10 (2.5e2 = 2.5 x 102 = 250).

complex (complex numbers) : are of the form a + bJ, where a and b are floats and J (or j) represents the square root of -1 (which is an imaginary number). The real part of the number is a, and the imaginary part is b. Complex numbers are not used much in Python programming.

Number Type Conversion

Python converts numbers internally in an expression containing mixed types to a common type for evaluation. But sometimes, you need to coerce a number explicitly from one type to another to satisfy the requirements of an operator or function parameter.

Type int(x) to convert x to a plain integer.

Type long(x) to convert x to a long integer.

Type float(x) to convert x to a floating-point number.

Type complex(x) to convert x to a complex number with real part x and imaginary part zero.

Type complex(x, y) to convert x and y to a complex number with real part x and imaginary part y. x and y are numeric expressions

Mathematical Functions
Python includes following functions that perform mathematical calculations.

Function Returns (description)
abs(x)

The absolute value of x: the (positive) distance between x and zero.

ceil(x)

The ceiling of x: the smallest integer not less than x

cmp(x, y)

-1 if x < y, 0 if x == y, or 1 if x > y

exp(x)

The exponential of x: ex

fabs(x)

The absolute value of x.

floor(x)

The floor of x: the largest integer not greater than x

log(x)

The natural logarithm of x, for x> 0

log10(x)

The base-10 logarithm of x for x> 0 .

max(x1, x2,...)

The largest of its arguments: the value closest to positive infinity

min(x1, x2,...)

The smallest of its arguments: the value closest to negative infinity

modf(x)

The fractional and integer parts of x in a two-item tuple. Both parts have the same sign as x. The integer part is returned as a float.

pow(x, y)

The value of x**y.

round(x [,n])

x rounded to n digits from the decimal point. Python rounds away from zero as a tie-breaker: round(0.5) is 1.0 and round(-0.5) is -1.0.

sqrt(x)

The square root of x for x > 0

Python interpreter

You can download Python interpreter here:
https://www.python.org/downloads

The Python interpreter is a command line program:

Python programs are simply a collection of text files. If you want something more sophisticated than notepad for editing, you will need a Python IDE (recommend). A Python IDE will make programming Python easier.

Python IDE

An IDE generally supports listing all program files, syntax highlighting and other features. There are a few Python IDEs y ou could choose from:

* PyDev
* Komodo Edit
* PyCharm
* Atom with Python plugin

Scope and Lifetime of variables

Scope of a variable is the portion of a program where the variable is recognized. Parameters and variables defined inside a function is not visible from outside. Hence, they have a local scope.

Lifetime of a variable is the period throughout which the variable exits in the memory. The lifetime of variables inside a function is as long as the function executes.

They are destroyed once we return from the function. Hence, a function does not remember the value of a variable from its previous calls.

Here is an example to illustrate the scope of a variable inside a function.

```
def my_func():
x = 10
print("Value inside function:",x)

x = 20

my_func()
print("Value outside function:",x)
```

Output

Value inside function: 10
Value outside function: 20

Here, we can see that the value of x is 20 initially. Even though the function my_func() changed the value of x to 10, it did not effect the value outside the function.

This is because the variable x inside the function is different (local to the function) from the one outside. Although they have same names, they are two different variables with different scope.

On the other hand, variables outside of the function are visible from inside. They have a global scope.

We can read these values from inside the function but cannot change (write) them. In order to modify the value of variables outside the function, they must be declared as global variables using the keyword global.

Types of Functions

Basically, we can divide functions into the following two types:

1. Built-in functions - Functions that are built into Python.

2. User-defined functions - Functions defined by the users themselves.

Python Objects and Class

In this section, you'll learn about the core functionality of Python, Python objects and classes. You'll learn what a class is, how to create it and use it in your program.

Python is an object oriented programming language. Unlike procedure oriented programming, where the main emphasis is on functions, object oriented programming stress on objects.

Object is simply a collection of data (variables) and methods (functions) that act on those data. And, class is a blueprint for the object.

We can think of class as a sketch (prototype) of a house. It contains all the details about the floors, doors, windows etc. Based on these descriptions we build the house. House is the object.

As, many houses can be made from a description, we can create many objects from a class. An object is also called an instance of a class and the process of creating this object is called instantiation.

Defining a Class in Python

Like function definitions begin with the keyword def, in Python, we define a class using the keyword class.

The first string is called docstring and has a brief description about the class. Although not mandatory, this is recommended.

Here is a simple class definition.

```
class MyNewClass:
    '''This is a docstring. I have created a new class'''
    pass
```

A class creates a new local namespace where all its attributes are defined. Attributes may be data or functions.

There are also special attributes in it that begins with double underscores (__). For example, __doc__ gives us the docstring of that class.

As soon as we define a class, a new class object is created with the same name. This class object allows us to access the different attributes as well as to instantiate new objects of that class.

```
class MyClass:
"This is my second class"
a = 10
def func(self):

print('Hello')

# Output:
10
print(MyClass.a)

# Output: <function MyClass.func at 0x0000000003079BF8>

print(MyClass.func)
# Output: 'This is my second class'
```

Creating an Object in Python

We saw that the class object could be used to access different attributes.

It can also be used to create new object instances (instantiation) of that class. The procedure to create an object is similar to a function call.

```
>>> ob = MyClass()
```

This will create a new instance object named ob. We can access attributes of objects using the object name prefix.

Attributes may be data or method. Method of an object are corresponding functions of that class. Any function object that is a class attribute defines a method for objects of that class.

This means to say, since MyClass.func is a function object (attribute of class), ob.func will be a method object.

```
class MyClass:
"This is my second class"

a = 10

def func(self):

print('Hello')

# create a new MyClass

ob = MyClass()

# Output: <function MyClass.func at 0x00000000335B0D0>
```

print(MyClass.func)

Output: <bound method MyClass.func of <__main__.MyClass object at 0x000000000332DEF0>>

print(ob.func)

You may have noticed the self parameter in function definition inside the class but, we called the method simply as ob.func() without any arguments. It still worked.

This is because, whenever an object calls its method, the object itself is passed as the first argument. So, ob.func() translates into MyClass.func(ob).

In general, calling a method with a list of n arguments is equivalent to calling the corresponding function with an argument list that is created by inserting the method's object before the first argument.

For these reasons, the first argument of the function in class must be the object itself. This is conventionally called self. It can be named otherwise but we highly recommend to follow the convention.

Now you must be familiar with class object, instance object, function object, method object and their differences.

Constructors in Python

Class functions that begins with double underscore (__) are called special functions as they have special meaning.

Of one particular interest is the __init__() function. This special function gets called whenever a new object of that class is instantiated.

This type of function is also called constructors in Object Oriented Programming (OOP). We normally use it to initialize all the variables.

```
class ComplexNumber:

    def __init__(self,r = 0,i = 0):

        self.real = r

        self.imag = i

    def getData(self):

        print("{0}+{1}j".format(self.real,self.imag))

# Create a new ComplexNumber object

c1 = ComplexNumber(2,3)

# Call getData() function
```

```
# Output: 2+3j

c1.getData()

# Create another ComplexNumber object

# and create a new attribute 'attr'

c2 = ComplexNumber(5)

c2.attr = 10

# Output: (5, 0, 10)

print((c2.real, c2.imag, c2.attr))

# but c1 object doesn't have attribute 'attr'
# AttributeError: 'ComplexNumber' object has no attribute 'attr'
c1.attr
```

In the above example, we define a new class to represent complex numbers. It has two functions, __init__() to initialize the variables (defaults to zero) and getData() to display the number properly.

An interesting thing to note in the above step is that attributes of an object can be created on the fly. We created a new attribute attr for object c2 and we read it as well. But this did not create that attribute for object c1.

Deleting Attributes and Objects

Any attribute of an object can be deleted anytime, using the del statement. Try the following on the Python shell to see the output.

```
>>> c1 = ComplexNumber(2,3)
>>> del c1.imag
>>> c1.getData()
Traceback (most recent call last):
...
AttributeError: 'ComplexNumber' object has no attribute
'imag'
```

```
>>> del ComplexNumber.getData
>>> c1.getData()
Traceback (most recent call last):
...
AttributeError: 'ComplexNumber' object has no attribute
'getData'
```

We can even delete the object itself, using the del statement.

```
>>> c1 = ComplexNumber(1,3)
>>> del c1
>>> c1
Traceback (most recent call last):
...
NameError: name 'c1' is not defined
```

Actually, it is more complicated than that. When we do c1 = ComplexNumber(1,3), a new instance object is created in memory and the name c1 binds with it.

On the command del c1, this binding is removed and the name c1 is deleted from the corresponding namespace. The object however continues to exist in memory and if no other name is bound to it, it is later automatically destroyed.

This automatic destruction of unreferenced objects in Python is also called garbage collection.

Print Function and Strings

The print function in Python is a function that outputs to your console window whatever you say you want to print out. At first blush, it might appear that the print function is rather useless for programming, but it is actually one of the most widely used functions in all of python. The reason for this is that it makes for a great debugging tool.

"Debugging" is the term given to the act of finding, removing, and fixing errors and mistakes within code.

If something isn't acting right, you can use the print function to print out what is happening in the program. Many times, you expect a certain variable to be one thing, but you cannot see what the program sees. If you print out the variable, you might see that what you thought was, was not.

Next up, strings, what are they? Strings are just "strings" of text, hence the name. Strings are a type of data. Another type of data is integers.

Here are some examples:

```
print('Single Quotes')
print("double quotes")
```

We're printing out a string. Notice that the quotes are single quotes. You can use single quotes or double quotes, but they need to be used together.

While we're talking about strings and the print function, it would be useful to discuss concatenation. Concatenation just means the combination of things. You can use the "+" or the "," to join strings together. If you use a ",", then you will have a space in between the strings you joined. If you use a "+", then the strings will be strung together with no space. You will need to add one if you wanted.

If you use the "+" to join integers and floats together, then you will perform an arithmetic operation. If you use the ",", then it will print them out separately, with a space.

```
print('can do this',5)

print('cannot do this:'+5)
```

You cannot use the "+" to join strings with ints or floats, you must use the ",".

It is also important to bring up how to put quotes within strings. You can either put double quotes inside single quotes, singles inside doubles, or use the "\" backslash. The \ character is known as an escape character, and it will "escape" the characteristic of the following character and just take on the 'visual' aspect of it.

The purpose of the "escape character" is to escape various characteristics for characters. For example, a quotation, ", in a string might wreak havoc. Take for example: x = "He said, "Hello there!" "

Yeah, that's going to be a problem. There are obviously many options to avoid this specific problem, but one of them would be to use an escape character:

```
x = "He said, \"Hello there!\" "
```

If you do a print(x), you will not see the escape characters, and you will see the quotes. Sometimes you want to show the escape character as well:

```
x = "An escape character is a \"
```

How might you solve that?
Here are some examples of quotation rules:

```
print('Can't do this')

print('you\'ll have success here')

print("you'll have success here too")
```

It is also important to bring up how to put quotes within strings. You can either put double quotes inside single quotes, singles inside doubles, or use the "\" backslash. The \ character is known as an "escape" character, and it will "escape" the characteristic of the following character and just take on the 'visual' aspect of it.

Math basics with Python 3

Math is a pretty popular topic, so we should probably learn how to do it in Python 3. Luckily for us, math is so very popular that it works extremely simply.

1+3

Here, we have some simple addition, the returned number is 4.

4*4

Next up, multiplication, fancy stuff! The return is 16.

5-2

Subtraction, even fancier. Return will be 3

5/2

Division, now this is actually fancy, based on Python's history.

In Python 2, the division does not necessarily work in the way expected. If you divide two whole numbers, you will be returned a whole number. You must divide one of the numbers as a float in order to get a proper return. This was changed in Python 3+, and now you always get expected division, yay!

```
#exponents
 4**4
```

There is another way to do exponents, but this works just fine, and is a familiar syntax for it.

That's it for basic math. It really is quite simple. Math is quite integral to a lot of programs, so it is very nice that it is kept simple enough.

Variables, what they are, and how to use them

In almost every single Python program you write, you will have variables. Variables act as placeholders for data. They can aid in short hand, as well as with logic, as variables can change, hence their name.

Variables help programs become much more dynamic, and allow a program to always reference a value in one spot, rather than the programmer needing to repeatedly type it out, and, worse, change it if they decide to use a different definition for it.

Variables can be called just about whatever you want. You wouldn't want them to conflict with function names, and they also cannot start with a number.

You want to be careful what you name variables, classes (discussed later), and functions (discussed later), so that they do not have the same names as eachother.

For example, you have leared about the print function. What if you go and define a variable named print?

Say, for example, you do:

```
print = print("Uh oh!")
```

Now you have a variable and a function named print, which can cause trouble down the road!

```
exampleVar = 55
print(exampleVar)
```

In this case, we will have a 55 printed out to console. So, in this case, we were able to store an integer to our variable.

```
cannotDo = Hey!
```

Hey! is not a valid datatype, and this will throw an error. You would need to throw quotes around the string.

```
canDo = 'Hey!'
print(canDo)
```

This is acceptable.

```
canContainOperations = 5/4
print(canContainOperations)
```

Here, we can see that we were even able to store the result of a calculation to our variable.

We can even store a variable to our variable, or an operation with our variables to a variable. Something like var3 = (var2/var1) would work. You can store other things, like functions, as well to variables. More on that later!

Try playing with variables in the console provided above, or via your own Python installation.

Global and Local Variables Python Tutorial

In this tutorial we're going to now discuss the concept of global and local variables.

When users begin using functions, they can quickly become confused when it comes to global and local variables... getting a the dreaded variable is not defined even when they clearly see that it is... or so they think.

These terms of global and local correspond to a variable's reach within a script or program. A global variable is one that can be accessed anywhere. A local variable is the opposite, it can only be accessed within its frame. The difference is that global variables can be accessed locally, but not modified locally inherently.

A local variable cannot be accessed globally, inherently. Now, dont worry about committing that to memory right now, I think it makes a lot more sense when you just see and do it, so let's do that.

this variable has no parent function, but is actually NOT a global variable.

it just so happens that it is committed to memory before the function is called

```
# so we are able to iterate, or call it out, but we cannot do much else.

x = 6

def example():
    print(x)
    # z, however, is a local variable.
    z = 5
    # this works
    print(z)

example()
# this does not, which often confuses people, because z has been defined
# and successfully even was called... the problem is that it is a local
# variable only, and you are attempting to access it globally.

print(z)
```

Here, we can see that we are able to access the x variable. We then defined and print out the z variable. We can then call the function, and all seems well. When we go to reference the z variable however, we have trouble. The z variable is local to the example function.

Let's look at another example:

```
x = 6

def example2():
    # works
    print(x)
    print(x+5)

    # but then what happens when we go to modify:
    x+=6

    # so there we attempted to take the x var and add 6 to it... but now
    # we are told that we cannot, as we're referencing the variable before
    # its assignment.
```

Here, again, we are able to reference x, we are even able to print x+6... but we are not allowed to modify x.

What if we'd like to modify x? Well, then we need to use global!

```
x = 6

def example3():
    # what we do here is defined x as a global variable.
    global x
```

```
    # now we can:
    print(x)
    x+=5
    print(x)
```

Now we're cooking! The problem here is that some people do not like the idea at all of using global variables. How do we get around using them and referencing them locally?

```
x = 6

def example4():
    globx = x
    # now we can:
    print(globx)
    globx+=5
    print(globx)
```

We are able to do the above, by assigning the value that we can reference to a local variable, then doing what we want with it from there.

Another choice you might have, as suggested by one of my viewers is the following:

```
x = 6
def example(x):

    print(x)
    x+=5
    print(x)
    return x

x = example(x)
print(x)
```

In the above example, we have the function modifying x. It may appear somewhat confusing since x is being used in multiple locations, so maybe a more clear example is something like:

```
x = 6
def example(modify):

    print(modify)
    modify+=5
    print(modify)
    return modify

x = example(x)
print(x)
```

So, you can better visualize this function as a "modification" function, where it modifies the variable you pass through. Besides the definition of this function, you only need to reassign the variable you want to change as the function with that variable as the parameter.

Appending Files

Now we get to appending a file in python. I will just state again that writing will clear the file and write to it just the data you specify in the write operation. Appending will simply take what was already there, and add the new data to it.

That said, when you actually go to add to the file, you will still use ".write." You only specify that you will be appending instead of writing when you open the file and specify your intentions.

Let's look at an example:

```
# so here, generally it can be a good idea to start with a newline, since
# otherwise it will append data on the same line as the file left off.
# you might want that, but I'll use a new line.
# another option used is to first append just a simple newline
# then append what you want.
appendMe = '\nNew bit of information'

appendFile = open('exampleFile.txt','a')
appendFile.write(appendMe)
appendFile.close()
```

What will happen here is, if exampleFile.txt already exists, the appendMe line will be added to it. If that file does not already exist, then it will be created.

Reading from Files

Now that we know how to write and append to files, we might want to learn how to read data from files into the Python program. Doing this is quite simple, and has very similar syntax.

```
# similar syntax as you've seen, 'r' for read. You can just throw a .read() at
# the end, and you get:
readMe = open('exampleFile.txt','r').read()
print(readMe)
```

Often times, people are reading something with many lines into memory. Maybe it's a list of names, or something like that. We can then use ".readlines()" to help us split all of this up into a Python list for us.

```
# this will instead read the file into a python list.
readMe = open('exampleFile.txt','r').readlines()
print(readMe)
```

Getting User Input

For a simple text-based GUI (graphical user interface), it can sometimes be useful to allow for a user to enter some input into the program while it runs. Using Python 3's "input" function, we can do that.

In time, you may want to eventually learn how to make GUIs in windows, but you will still find yourself needing raw input from time to time, like text fields, even in these sorts of GUIs.

```
x = input('What is your name?: ')
print('Hello',x)
```

Statistics Module

Since Python is such a popular programming language for data analysis, it only makes sense that it comes with a statistics module. Sadly, this is not available in Python 2.7, but that's okay because we're in Python 3!

The statistics module comes with an assortment of goodies: Mean, median, mode, standard deviation, and variance.

These are all fairly straight forward to use, here and some simple examples:

```
import statistics

example_list = [5,2,5,6,1,2,6,7,2,6,3,5,5]

x = statistics.mean(example_list)
print(x)

y = statistics.median(example_list)
print(y)

z = statistics.mode(example_list)
print(z)
```

```
a = statistics.stdev(example_list)
print(a)

b = statistics.variance(example_list)
print(b)
```

We've not gone much over importing things in Python, so I've kept this basic. As you can see, you just simply pass a list through the module's function, and you're output is the answer. Here, we're saving the output to a variable, and then we're just printing out the variable. In normal circumstances, you'd probably continue doing things with it.

Here, we've seen how simple importing and using modules can be, but there are a lot of other options when it comes to how we import things.

Module import Syntax

Now that we've used a module, statistics, it would be a good time to explain some import syntax practices. As with many things in programming, there are many ways to import modules, but there are certainly some best practices.

So first, when you import a module, you are basically loading that module into memory. Think of a module like a script. Many if not most modules are just a single python script. So, when you go to import it, you use the file name. This can help keep code clean and easy to read. Many python developers just program everything in 1 script. Other developers, say from a language like java are going to be very used to doing lots of imports with a file for each type of job that's happening. Just like there are many ways to import, there are many more ways to program.

So let's talk about basic importing:

import statistics

Above, we have referenced the statistics module and loaded it into memory under the statistics object. This will allow us to reference any of the functions within the statistics module. To do so, we will need to mention statistics, followed by a period, then the function name. A simple exhibition of the mean function from statistics could look like this:

```
import statistics

example_list = [5,2,5,6,1,2,6,7,2,6,3,5,5]

print(statistics.mean(example_list))
```

The generated output from this will be the mean, or average, of the list.

That is the simplest way to import and use modules, but there are many other methods. In the video, we cover each one specifically, but here are a bunch of examples:

Sometimes, however, you will see people use the "as" statement in their imports. This will allow you to basically rename the module to whatever you want. People generally do this to shorten the name of the module. Matplotlib.pyplot is often imported as plt and numpy is often imported as np, for example.

```
import statistics as s

print(s.mean(example_list))
```

Above, we've imported statistics as the letter 's.' This means whenever we wish to reference the statistics module, we just need to type 's' instead of statistics.

What if you don't even want to type that S though? Well there's an app for that!

You can just import each function within the module you plan to use:

```
from statistics import mean
# so here, we've imported the mean function only.
print(mean(example_list))

# and again we can do as
from statistics import mean as m
print(m(example_list))
```

Above, you can see that we no longer had to type any reference to the statistics module, then you saw that we could even import the functions "as" something else.

What about more functions?

```
from statistics import mean, median
# here we imported 2 functions.
print(median(example_list))
```

What if we want to use the as as well?

```
from statistics import mean as m, median as d

print(m(example_list))
print(d(example_list))
```

What if we want to just import everything from statistics like we did initially, but we don't want to type the statistics because we have fat fingers and this will just slow us down?.

```
from statistics import *

print(mean(example_list))
```

Making your own Modules

Modules are often confusing to people who are first getting started in Python, and they don't have to be! For the most part, modules are just Python scripts that are stored in your Lib or Lib/site-packages folder, or local to the script being run. That's it. The installation of *most* modules is simply the moving of the module's files into these directories. It's very basic. You should be able to, after watching this quick series, just simply download the source code of the module that you are looking to employ, and move the source code yourself to the packages directory.

My aim here is to show how you can create your very own module and where you can put it so you can import it. Hopefully with this information, you can better understand how modules work, that you can edit modules, and what to do if you only have the source code for the module you are wanting.

To do this, the example module that we create is called examplemod.py, and within it is just the following:

```
def ex(data):
    print(data)
```

That's it! We just put a function in there that, when called, will just print out the parameter.

Now, we just need to import and use that.

Doing so is as simple as:

```
import examplemod
examplemod.ex('test')
```

To do this, the examplemod.py file must be in the same directory as your running-program, or in your Python packages directory. If you are on a windows machine, this will be C:/python34/Lib/site-packages/

Hopefully this can help you see that there really is no "magic" behind most modules. You can look through your own standard library that comes with Python in the /Lib/ directory. This is where all of your standard library modules are. Just take a peak through them to see most of them are just simple Python scripts. There are some more complex modules out there, but the vast majority of Python modules are just simple scripts, sometimes they are "packages" where there are many scripts within a folder, but this is still all it is.

Python Lists vs Tuples

Our focus here is the difference between Python lists and tuples. Often confused, due to their similarities, these two structures are substantially different.

A tuple is an assortment of data, separated by commas, which makes it similar to the Python list, but a tuple is fundamentally different in that a tuple is "immutable." This means that it cannot be changed, modified, or manipulated. A tuple is typically used specifically because of this property. A popular use for this is sequence unpacking, where we want to store returned data to some specified variables. Something like:

```
def example():
    return 15, 12

x, y = example()
print(x,y)

# in the above case, we have used a tuple and cannot modify it... and
# we definitely do not want to!
```

If you notice, the tuple had no brackets around it at all. If there are no encasing brackets or braces of any type, then

Python will recognize the data as a tuple. Tuples also can have curved brackets like "(" or ")"

Next, we have the far more popular Python list. To define a list, we use square brackets. A Python list acts very much like an array in other languages like php.

Here's an example of a list and an example use:

```
x = [1,3,5,6,2,1,6]

'''
You can then reference the whole list like:
'''
print(x)

# or a single element by giving its index value.
# index values start at 0 and go up by 1 each time

print(x[0],x[1])
```

List Manipulation

This section of the ebook covers list manipulation. This includes adding things to the end, inserting them into specific positions, removing things, finding data, counting the number of occurrences, sorting, and reversing the data.

All of the above are very common operations with lists, and all of them are built into Python 3 for ease of use.

Keep in mind that lists are mutable, and using these functions change the list.

Here is some example code of list manipulation:

Since lists are mutable, this means that we will be using lists for things where we might intend to manipulate the list of data, so how can we do that? Turns out we can do all sorts of things.

We can add, remove, count, sort, search, and do quite a few other things to python lists.

```
# first we need an example list:
x = [1,6,3,2,6,1,2,6,7]
# lets add something.
# we can do .append, which will add something to the end of the list, like:
x.append(55)
print(x)
```

Above, we took a list, and added to the end of the list with .append. Remember append with files? Same thing, .append() will add to the end of a list.

What if you have an exact place that you'd like to put something in a list, instead of just at the very end?

```
x.insert(2,33)
print(x)
```

Here we say that we want to insert, at the index of 2, the number 33. The reason that went in the 3rd place, again, is because we start at the zero element, then go 1, 2...etc with lists.

Now we can remove things. .remove() will remove the first instance of the value in the list. If it doesn't exist, there will be an error:

```
x.remove(6)
print(x)
```

Next, remember how we can reference an item by index in a list? like:

```
print(x[5])
```

Well, we can also search for this index, like so:

```
print(x.index(1))
```

Now here, we can see that it actually returned a 0, meaning the first element was a 1... when we knew there was another with an index of 5. So, instead we might want to know before-hand how many examples there are.

```
print(x.count(1))
```

We see there are actually 2 of them

We can also sort the list:

```
x.sort()
print(x)
```

What if these were strings? like:

```
y = ['Jan','Dan','Bob','Alice','Jon','Jack']
y.sort()
print(y)
y.reverse()
print(y)
```

Multi-dimensional lists

Multi dimensional lists are lists within lists, or lists within lists within lists... you get the point. It can get very confusing very fast, but it is good to know that it is an option. Usually a dictionary will be the better choice rather than a multi-dimensional list in Python, but, if you are familiar with multi-dimensional arrays in other languages, you might want to continue that concept in Python.

Lists that we have covered so far have all been 1 dimensional, but you can have lists within lists within lists within lists if you want.

We already know how to reference elements in a list, we can do:

```
x = [[2,6],[6,2],[8,2],[5,12]]
print(x[2])
```

We can also take this deeper since we have more dimensions now:

```
print(x[2][1])
```

This can go on indefinitely with very thick lists. You might see how this can quickly get messy, so let's consider how to properly display lists in code that have many dimensions. You might not typically hard code multi-dimensional lists, but there are some instances where you will.

```
y = [[5,2],
    [6,2],
    [3,1],
    [12,6]
   ]
```

This is slightly cleaner, and python automatically understands it:

```
print(y)
```

Reading CSV files in Python

Let's cover how to read CSV data in from a file and then use it in Python. For this, we use the csv module. CSV literally stands for comma separated variable, where the comma is what is known as a "delimiter." While you can also just simply use Python's split() function, to separate lines and data within each line, the CSV module can also be used to make things easy.

Here is the sample code

Example CSV file data:

```
1/2/2014,5,8,red
1/3/2014,5,2,green
1/4/2014,9,1,blue
```

Next, let's cover the reading of CSV files into memory:

```
import csv

with open('example.csv') as csvfile:
    readCSV = csv.reader(csvfile, delimiter=',')
    for row in readCSV:
        print(row)
        print(row[0])
        print(row[0],row[1],row[2],)
```

Above, we've shown how to open a CSV file and read each row, as well as reference specific data on each row.

Next, we will show how to pull out specific data from the spreadsheet and save it to a list variable:

```
import csv

with open('example.csv') as csvfile:
    readCSV = csv.reader(csvfile, delimiter=',')
    dates = []
    colors = []
    for row in readCSV:
        color = row[3]
        date = row[0]

        dates.append(date)
        colors.append(color)
```

```
    print(dates)
    print(colors)
```

Once we have this data, what can we do with it? Maybe we are curious about what color something was on a specific date.

```
import csv

with open('example.csv') as csvfile:
    readCSV = csv.reader(csvfile, delimiter=',')
    dates = []
    colors = []
    for row in readCSV:
        color = row[3]
        date = row[0]

        dates.append(date)
        colors.append(color)

    print(dates)
    print(colors)

    # now, remember our lists?

    whatColor = input('What color do you wish to know
the date of?:')
    coldex = colors.index(whatColor)
```

```
theDate = dates[coldex]
print('The date of',whatColor,'is:',theDate)
```

Simple enough! If we enter something that doesn't exist, we get an ugly error.

Try and Except Error handling

Let's cover the Try and Except statements, which are used for error handling. These statements work similarly to the if-else, where if the Try runs, the except will not run. If the Try fails, then the exception will run with the error that was just generated in the try. Try and Except is mainly used to handle failures in code, which result in errors. With handling exceptions, you can keep your code running when it would otherwise grind to a catastrophic halt from an error. You can also use error handling to log problems in your code, or to even attempt to remedy the problem as a part of the program.

Here is the sample data from the CSV file that we are reading from:

```
1/2/2014,5,8,red
1/3/2014,5,2,green
1/4/2014,9,1,blue
```

Now we need to learn how to handle errors in Python. As you can see, if you do not have any error handling, your program or script will just stop completely. This is not likely to be desired! First, we want to figure out how to handle errors, which is really just treating the symptom to the problem, not really solving the problem. Then, we want to learn how to avoid these sorts of problems to begin with, using proper logic in our programs.

Here is the sample code that matches the video:

```
import csv

with open('example.csv') as csvfile:
    readCSV = csv.reader(csvfile, delimiter=',')
    dates = []
    colors = []
    for row in readCSV:
        color = row[3]
        date = row[0]

        dates.append(date)
        colors.append(color)

    print(dates)
    print(colors)
```

The above is the same, but here's where the code changes. We can put the "try" statement in quite a few places to solve our problem. I like to put the try statement in front of any new "block" of logic. Here, our logic block begins by asking the user to enter some input. This should immediately be a cause for concern, since we're opening a "door" to our program, and we might receive some unwanted input.

A great example of this is input fields on websites. Say you have a log-in with username and password field. Generally, you expect the user to enter a username and a password. First off, they might enter a non-existent username and password. Either they do not have one, they forgot it, or accidentally made a mistake in the input.

Sometimes, input isn't as innocent as this, as people sometimes have more sinister intentions. Using what is known as SQL injection, hackers can attempt to either gain access to your database or administration, or even wreak havoc on your website by modifying or just plain dropping tables in your database. Instead of entering usernames and passwords, hackers can enter SQL queries. If not handled right, your back-end code might actually go to run the SQL statement the hacker intends. The basic SQL injection usually starts with closing off the SQL statement you intended to run from your field, then begins a brand new query from the field. It looks nothing like a username or a password to a person, but your system may still blindly run it. This is a prime example where not only error handling is necessary to know, but also proper logic is imperative.

```
try:
        whatColor = input('What color do you wish to
know the date of?:')
        coldex = colors.index(whatColor)
        theDate = dates[coldex]
```

```
        print('The date of',whatColor,'is:',theDate)

    # in python 2, this is read exception Exception, e. It's
just helpful
    # to know this for porting old scripts if you need to.


    except Exception as e:
        print(e)


    ''' So this will try a block of code, and, if there is an
exception, it
    will continue to run...
    '''
    print('Stilllllllll running though!')
```

This shown, we should always treat try and exception handling as a last resort, or a final point of failure. We should really instead code in a conditional before the exception is thrown, something like:

```
with open('example.csv') as csvfile:
    readCSV = csv.reader(csvfile, delimiter=',')
    dates = []
    colors = []
    for row in readCSV:
        color = row[3]
        date = row[0]
```

```
        dates.append(date)
        colors.append(color)

    print(dates)
    print(colors)

    # we could put the try anywhere. The weak point, however, starts
    # in my opinion immediately when we accept user input... no longer
    # is this is a closed-program, so I would personally code this block
    # here, but you could put the try right about the print statement
    # of where we search for the color and we KNOW it will throw an error
    # if not in the list.
    try:
        whatColor = input('What color do you wish to know the date of?:')

        if whatColor in colors:
            coldex = colors.index(whatColor)
            theDate = dates[coldex]
            print('The date of',whatColor,'is:',theDate)
        else:
            # now we can handle a specific scenario, instead
            # of handling it with a "catch-all" error.
            # now we have error handling and
```

```
            # proper logic. Yay.
            print('This color was not found.')

        # in python 2, this is read exception Exception, e. It's
just helpful
        # to know this for porting old scripts if you need to.


        except Exception as e:
            print(e)
```

Above, we've not only handled an error if we get one, but we also have coded in proper logic. Just as a quick note, the above logic will absolutely not stop an SQL injection. I am just using that as an example of why logic is necessary!

Also, it should be noted that you can stack exceptions to cover specific errors.

Multi-Line printing

The idea of multi-line printing in Python is to be able to easily print across multiple lines, while only using 1 print function, while also printing out exactly what you intend. Sometimes, when making something like a text-based graphical user interface, it can be quite tedious and challenging to make everything line up for you. This is where multi-line printing can be very useful.

```
print(
'''
This
is
a
test
'''
  )

print(
'''
So it works like a multi-line
comment, but it will print out.
```

You can make kewl designs like this:

```
==============
|             |
|             |
|     BOX     |
|             |
|             |
==============
'''
  )
```

Why Python Has Become an Industry Favorite Among Programmers

With the world stepping towards a new age of technology development, it isn't hard to imagine a future that will be full of screens. And if so be the case then, demand for people with strong programming skills will definitely rise with more number of people required to develop and support the applications. Python Training is always a good idea for those wishes to be a part of this constantly developing industry. Python language is not only easy to grasp, but emphasizes less on syntax which is why a few mistakes here and there doesn't give as much trouble as some other languages does.

What Makes Python a Preferred Choice Among Programmers?

Python happens to be an easy programming language which offers its support to various application types starting from education to scientific computing to web development. Tech giants like Google along with Instagram have also made use of Python and its popularity continues to rise. Discussed below are some of the advantages offered by Python:

First Steps in the World of Programming

Aspiring programmers can use Python to enter the programming world. Like several other programming languages such as Ruby, Perl, JavaScript, C#, C++, etc. Python is also object oriented based programming language. People who have thorough knowledge of Python can easily adapt to other environments. It is always recommended to acquire working knowledge so as to become aware of the methodologies that are used across different applications.

Simple and Easy to Understand and Code

Many people will agree to the fact that, learning and understanding a programming language isn't that exciting as compared to a tense baseball game. But, Python on the other hand was specifically developed keeping in mind newcomers.

Even to the eye of a layman, it will seem meaningful and easy to understand. Curly brackets and tiring variable declarations are not part of this programming language thus, making it a lot easier to learn language.

Getting Innovative

Python has helped in bringing real world and computing a lot close with it Raspberry Pi. This inexpensive, card-sized microcomputer helps tech enthusiasts to build various DIY stuffs like video gaming consoles, remote controlled cars and robots. Python happens to be the programming language that powers this microcomputer. Aspirants can select from different DIY projects available online and enhance their skills and motivations by completing such projects.

Python also Supports Web Development

With its huge capabilities, Python is also a favorite among web developers to build various types of web applications. The web application framework, Django has been developed using Python and serves as the foundation for popular websites like 'The Guardian', 'The NY Times', 'Pinterest' and more.

Python provides aspiring programmers a solid foundation based on which they can branch out to different fields. Python programming training ensures that students are able to use this highly potential programming language to the best of its capabilities in an exciting and fun way. Those who are keen to make a great career as software programmers are definite to find Python live up to their expectations.

What Are the Top 5 Reasons for Learning Python?

One of the most robust and dynamic programming languages being used today is Python. It stresses a lot on code readability, and because of its syntax as well as implementation, programmers have to write lesser codes in comparison to Java and C++.

Memory management in Python is done automatically and several standard libraries are available for the programmer here. After completing a certification course in Python training, a programmer can gain experience in various top IT companies.

Python programming supports numerous styles such as functional programming, imperative and object-oriented styles. Here are the top five reasons why a computer programmer must learn the Python language:

Ease of learning- Python has been created with the newcomer in mind. Completion of basic tasks requires less code in Python, compared to other languages. The codes are usually 3-5 times shorter than Java, and 5-10 times smaller than C++. Python codes are easily readable and with a little bit of knowledge, new developers can learn a lot by just looking at the code.

Highly preferred for web development- Python consists of an array of frameworks which are useful in designing a website. Among these frameworks, Django is the most popular one for python development. Due to these frameworks, web designing with Python has immense flexibility. The number of websites online today are close to 1 billion, and with the ever-increasing scope for more, it is natural that Python programming will continue to be an important skill for web developers.

Considered ideal for start-ups- Time and budget are vital constraints for any new product or service in a company, and more so if it is a startup. One can create a product that differentiates itself from the rest in any language. However, for quick development, less code and lesser cost, Python is the ideal language here. Python can easily scale up any complex application and also can be handled by a small team. Not only do you save resources, but you also get to develop applications in the right direction with Python.

Unlimited availability of resources and testing framework- Several resources for Python are available today, and these are also constantly being updated. As a result, it is very rare that a Python developer gets stuck. The vast standard library provides in-built functionalities. Its built in testing framework enables speedy workflows and less debugging time.

Fat paycheques- Today top IT companies such as Google, Yahoo, IBM and Nokia make use of Python. Among all programming languages, it has had amazing growth over the last few years.

Conclusion

Python is a terrific language. The syntax is simple and code length is short which makes is easy to understand and write.

If you are getting started in programming, Python is an awesome choice. You will be amazed how much you can do in Python once you know the basics.

Python provides aspiring programmers a solid foundation based on which they can branch out to different fields. Python programming training ensures that students are able to use this highly potential programming language to the best of its capabilities in an exciting and fun way. Those who are keen to make a great career as software programmers are definite to find Python live up to their expectations.

It's easy to overlook the fact that Python is a powerful language. Not only is it good for learning programming, it's also a good language to have in your arsenal. Change your idea into a prototype or create games or get started with data Science, Python can help you in everything to get started.

Python is a terrific language. The syntax is simple and code length is short which makes is easy to understand and write.

If you are getting started in programming, Python is an awesome choice. You will be amazed how much you can do in Python once you know the basics.

It's easy to overlook the fact that Python is a powerful language. Not only is it good for learning programming, it's also a good language to have in your arsenal. Change your idea into a prototype or create games or get started with data Science, Python can help you in everything to get started.

Thanks for reading

www.ingramcontent.com/pod-product-compliance
Lightning Source LLC
Chambersburg PA
CBHW070844070326
40690CB00009B/1696

9781545541180